Fundamentals
of
Sales

ISBN-13: 978-1523234943
ISBN-10: 1523234946

DEDICATION

As with everything I do, this work is dedicated first to
Christ, without whom I could do nothing;

to my wife, without whom I would do everything one
tenth as well;

to my daughter, whose existence is more inspiring
than the clearest fall day;

and to my mentors Mac and Chip, who have pushed
me to grow in all of the above.

CONTENTS

INTRODUCTION

I have a giant whiteboard in my home office. Around the edges, I have simple statements that I need to see every day until those statements become habits in my life. *It's all a jumble in your mind* was on my board for six months before I consistently wrote things down. *Businesses are people* was on my board for a year before I ingrained approaching opportunities as relationships to build.

That is what this book is intended to be; and I intentionally kept it short. Its purpose is to be read every six months or a year as a reminder of the most basic building blocks of relationships, until they're ingrained. There's no question that this is a journal of the things I have painfully learned about sales throughout my life so far and that I still struggle to remember every day.

This book is to acknowledge that there has always been, and always will be, business; that business is people who create value with their labor, and desire to trade it with others; to be a cause to remember that all business is predicated upon relationships; that there *are* fundamental principles that we as humans can adhere to no matter how the culture or the universe shifts so that we can create really excellent relationships and really excellent business.

PEOPLE ARE PEOPLE

The people who buy from me know me, and I know the people that I sell to.

We've all heard the term *customer*. Customer means "someone who purchases goods." If you provide something and someone pays for it then you have a customer. You might get paid for working a job or selling a product. Either way, customers are the recipients of our efforts: we spend our own resources to create value and then someone else sees that value and trades us some of their resources for it.

The most dangerous thing that we can do is to forget that the people on either end of these transactions *have names*. They have families, histories, lives and stories. The person who just walked into your store or landed on your website isn't your *customer*...he's Brian. Brian is looking for something to make his life different; he's looking for a gift for his wife. Brian likes to give gifts and his wife likes to get them. His wife, Allison, likes to get gifts from Brian because it lets her know that he's thinking about her. Now, he's in your store.

You don't know anything about Brian the first time he walks in or visits your website; but you have an opportunity each time you connect to establish that he's not a *customer* to you, he's **Brian**.

Similarly, my name is Nathan. While I am not the entirety of the companies I work for, or even those I've started, if you say something positive or negative about them then you are talking about me. The other day on the phone my support person's name was Kim. Whatever issue that I had, I was talking to Kim and I wanted to value her so that we could build a relationship and (hopefully) also take care of my issue. (We did.)

When people feel valued and they can tell, it makes their lives better. If we're being honest, that's why most of us do anything we do: to make life better.

KNOW YOUR PRODUCT

One of the most powerful and genuine of all sales techniques is to know your product.

It's been a common thing to hear in the last few decades that to be truly successful you must find your *niche*. You have to be an expert in your tiny, tiny section of the world. You can't just **be** an expert either, you need to position yourself as one as well. Whatever it takes, show that you're an expert!

So you might be shocked by how many people have no idea what they're selling. They don't understand the value of it, and they definitely don't understand why a potential customer would value it. Those same people are often confused about why, after pouring a lot of effort into a process, they still can't sell their product. I've been in this boat. I am still in that boat sometimes. Almost every time I come up with a new idea I'm in that boat for at least ten minutes; so, I practically live in that boat.

My wife and I recently watched a documentary called *Jiro dreams of Sushi* about

Master Sushi Chef Jiro Ono. Mr. Ono has been making Sushi for seventy years, and is considered to be the world's greatest Sushi Chef. He runs a restaurant that seats ten people at a time and charges a $250 per person minimum for a meal that is often eaten in *fifteen minutes*. Reservations are *required* and in the documentary when we see a man try to make a reservation for the same day he is told that he would have needed to make it a month ago.

Chef Ono's restaurant has a 3 Star Michelin rating. You probably know Michelin as a tire company. You may not have known that the company is over 100 years old and has been publishing travel guides most of its life. In the guides, they highlight restaurants and destinations worth visiting by giving them star ratings. The stars and guides are such a big deal that the yearly publishing of them in France has been equated to the Academy Awards. Media outlets go crazy talking about who might get a Michelin star. For perspective, at the beginning of 2016 there were 117 restaurants *in the world* that held 3 star ratings.

The legendary status of Jiro Ono is obviously because he's a master at his craft; however, what particularly inspired me were the various fish, shrimp, and rice vendors that we worked with. In the documentary they make no secret that the reason those vendors are used is because they know their products and know them intimately. In one scene the rice vendor almost flippantly mentions that the Grand Hyatt Hotel in Tokyo approached him to purchase his rice. His response? "I know this rice, and I know that Jiro can cook it correctly, and they can't. So this is Jiro's rice. Why would I sell it to them if they can't cook it?" During another moment, the shrimp vendor remarks "Each day, I look through the shrimp to find one that is worthy of Jiro." They trust each other to know exactly what will provide value and so each vendor offers his product unabashedly.

The other common theme the vendors shared, including Jiro himself, is that they know their product so well, they're never afraid to say, "This is *not* good." Which means that there is never a doubt in their minds that they're serving you the best. The best fish, the best rice. They absolutely believe that if they've determined it's valuable to you, that you would be crazy not to buy from them.

When someone really knows their product that well, that seems like a fair accusation.

REPEATED SMALL SALES
ARE THE BIG SALE

Picture this scenario:

A man walks into a cafe and sees a woman sitting at a table, reading a book by herself. He walks over and asks her about the book, remarking that he recognizes the author but hasn't seen this title before. She tells him a bit about the book, and he asks her a few questions about herself. They have a nice chat for a few minutes. The conversation is about ready to shut down when the man says, *"Hey, would you be my girlfriend?"*...

How this could go instead:

The conversation is about ready to shut down, and then the man says, "Hey, I've enjoyed chatting and I'd like to continue the conversation. Could I buy you a coffee soon?" Let's say the woman says yes, and they exchange contact information. After he leaves the cafe, the man shoots a text to the woman that simply has his

7

name and says, *"It was great to meet you and I'm looking forward to connecting again. How about you snag a look at your calendar and I'll call in a couple days?"* Then the man sends connection requests on Facebook, LinkedIn, follows her on Twitter, likes her Instagram posts, and tags her in his next four status updates...

How this could go instead:

A couple days pass and the man calls, he asks how she's doing and they chat for a second. He asks her if she knows a day that she's free and, let's say she tells him a day. He says great and that he's looking forward to it. Then the day happens: they meet and he buys coffee, they enjoy conversation and seem pretty compatible. Their time is winding down and the man says, *"This was great and I really enjoy spending time with you. There's a wine and art class happening at Studio 501 this Friday night, would you be interested in coming with me?"*

How likely do you think it is that the woman will say yes?

The whole point is that business is relationships; and relationships are built. Just like these scenarios, there's a moment when you'll have a chance to ask for the next level. You can either jump to the big sale or you can request that you take another step in building that relationship of attention and trust.

Every relationship is different, and sometimes you'll skip a few steps, while other times you'll get kicked off the path entirely; however, in general, relationships are built a little at a time. One small "sale" at a time, until it feels silly not to progress forward... and that's the big sale.

DOMLUVIT SE

In a plot twist that you could probably see coming, I'm now going to say something that will seem to contrast to what I just said. There is a skill that, in my own generation and those close to it, we have nearly lost: the ability to get everything set out on the table, all at once.

I do not mean in the example of the man and woman where the man approaches the big question during the first conversation. Often it makes no sense to jump all in right away. There are too many things that you don't even know yet.

What I do mean is that moment when the possibility of something more exists, but it's left alone. Or even more frustrating, when it is touched on and then left to hang in the air without action. Have you ever heard something that sounded like, "We should get together for coffee sometime!" and then absolutely nothing happens for months, or ever?

My friend Tom introduced me to this concept. Tom lived in the Czech Republic for almost twenty years, and his family can still speak Czech even though they've been primarily in the U.S. for a while now. I asked him one day if there were any phrases that exist in Czech that don't exist in English. He hardly needed to think about it before he said, *"Domluvit Se."* Apparently, it's a phrase that means "to figure something out completely, from beginning to end."

Let me show you how this would work in a real life situation: I'm sitting at a table in the café speaking with my friend Fred. You're passing our table and stop to talk to us because my friend Fred is your friend too! Fred introduces us and, after a minute of chatting, it becomes apparent that we have a few common interests. I look at you and say, "Domluvit se coffee?" You say, "that sounds great!" and then we stop right there, explain our basic reasons for connecting, decide if it's worth it, check our calendars, pick a time and date, and schedule it.

Wait… what!?

In general, in our society, we're not allowed to do this. We have to go through the pain of being vague instead. The reason we have to go through this pain is because we are afraid of doing what the man who proposed on the first date did: ask too much too fast. (To be brutally honest, we're also terrified of rejection.) This societal understanding that we're just telling polite lies is not only disingenuous, it's downright inefficient.

Most of the time in the real world, the scenario looks like this: I look at you and say, "Want to grab coffee sometime?" And you say, "That would be great!" and I say, "Great, I'll connect with you." Now that we've determined the *very idea* of meeting is alright, I'm left with this arduous task of sending you a follow-up e-mail or LinkedIn message the next time I get to my computer, but not until I check my calendar and stress over which times might be best for you, and whether it's acceptable to use a smiley face emoji in my message. Then you get the request and think, "What? He actually wants to go get coffee?" So you leave the e-mail in your inbox (gah!) and let your mind stew for the next twenty hours over whether it's going to be a waste of your time or not, until finally you feel obligated enough to at least tell me you're busy at those times and offer a different one that feels convenient. But then I accept the time you gave me and now you have *another* meeting and **why are we even meeting?**

Or we could have just figured all of that out in two minutes at the coffee shop the first time.

Don't go for the BIG SALE because that's not relational. But don't break the sales down so small that victories start feeling like a chore.

Domluvit se, and don't be afraid.

**It's pronounced "Dome-loov-it say".

INBOUND/OUTBOUND

Originally this chapter was one of the longest. I had so many thoughts to put here that I wasn't sure how to make it reasonable. Then I had a conversation with someone I'm coaching through starting a cafe. He's a smart guy, and a really hard worker. The other day we were talking about his social media, and I was asking about his inbound/outbound marketing mix. He just said, "What do those terms even mean, and what's the point? Shouldn't I just...have a Facebook?"

I blinked and realized that everything I was getting ready to say about strategy was probably completely irrelevant, and he would understand everything he needed to know if I just told him the base purpose of each and what they looked like. So, here's what I said:

Inbound Marketing: You put something out for people to see and hope they like it and walk in the door. Having a sign outside is Inbound Marketing. It is not specifically about the internet. Put something that talks about your business in a place you think people will see it and hope they'll be interested enough to call you. That's it.

Outbound Marketing: Outbound marketing is finding individual people and giving them information about what you do. Starting conversations with people on purpose to talk about your products, mailing postcards, handing out flyers, sending a resume, attending networking events - that's outbound marketing. That's it.

I ended up cutting roughly three pages out of this section because after that conversation I realized the fundamentals of these things are not that complicated. Go figure.

Now, there's a ton to talk about when it comes to strategy and message and audience and innovative methods and all that jazz. But the reality is, if you first know what you're trying to do, you'll be in a much better place to do it. Specific methods for your individual situation should come AFTER that.

P.S. I was right, he had a great strategy within like five minutes.

INSIDE/OUTSIDE

This will have a similar flavor to inbound/outbound marketing. I've also included a matrix to showcase all four areas and also how a few simple squares can challenge you to grow.

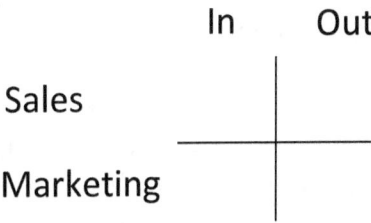

Inside Sales and Outside Sales are literal terms. You're literally doing sales from <u>inside</u> the office, or <u>outside</u> of it. As our ability to communicate without being face-to-face has increased, the amount of time we're willing to spend in-person with people whom we do not know has decreased.

So, inside sales has blossomed as a more than viable way to sell products and services. Using every resource at their fingertips, the inside salesperson sends email, Facebook and LinkedIn messages, and then some more emails. On increasingly rare occasions, they even call.

But no matter how educated we become on our own time, and no matter how fantastic we can make our online demos or emails, there will always be something special about human interaction. Having a real person stand in front of you and say, "I've learned about your life and I also know about this service and, wow, they would make a great pair!" can't be replicated or faked. There's a connection in shaking a hand and reading an expression… because we're still people. We're all still people.

Honestly, there's something to say about outside sales simply because it's one of the only ways you can be in the right place at the right time, in person. I read a story about a girl scout who sold cookies outside of a marijuana dispensary and once went through 117 boxes in two hours. Daymond John, who we know as the CEO of FUBU and of Shark Tank fame, got his start by standing outside of a mall and selling hats he had sewn by hand. He sold $800 worth of hats in a single day. There are some things that can only be done by being there in person.

In each industry, the most effective way to communicate about your product is different, and that's where the simple matrix comes in. These are the methods we use to let other people know that we have something valuable to trade with them. There are a lot of different specific methods that might make sense for your situation, but they're all going to fall into one of these four categories.

PLANS MAKE SALES EASY

Since I talk about the marketing and sales matrix all the time, I find that it occasionally leads me to doing a project. This year I took on a project to develop a marketing and sales plan. As I chatted with others about that project throughout the next month or so, it ended up turning into four projects. I was now designing plans for four different companies, one of which was my own!

Outside sales and marketing firms were something that my new clients and I had all looked into, but given up on. When I spoke with marketing firms I always left the conversation feeling like they were very skilled at their specific methods, but I also felt that each one needed my direction and planning in order to enact their methods. Well, before I had the marketing/sales matrix, and even for a while afterwards, I wasn't sure what my plan should be. I wasn't sure where to focus my efforts and I just gave up trying to use an outside firm. I've known a lot of small business owners who have the same issue with employees in general, trying to hire people they can barely afford but then just telling them to, "Go figure it out, that's what I did!" and then becoming frustrated when it's not working out like their foggy vision said it could.

Well, since none of us were sure how to direct *any* team in a way that made us feel confident, none of us had ended up hiring anyone else either. We all knew we needed to be marketing to generate awareness, and running some sort of sales method, but there still wasn't anyone working on that and no clear plan for what to do about it.

I decided to approach the whole issue from another angle: I started dreaming about what *every company* should be able to accomplish with their marketing planning. By creating a tool to do it, and testing it myself, I came up with a twelve-step template to build marketing plans very simply. I felt that if I could make something simple enough for me to build a plan from, it would help other companies facing all the same issues. To be honest, and somewhat to my surprise, I found that the template was pretty easy to come up with and very easy to implement for others. It didn't even matter if the company was large or small, the twelve steps I found really did seem to tackle all the necessary areas. Go figure that there would be some standard questions, right? Each of the questions focuses on something very basic that doesn't change. Time, people, place, desired effect. In fact, my company's weekly newsletter

Doing Business Better is one thing that came from using the plan for myself. Then, writing that newsletter led me to having the confidence and starting material to write this book. So it's actually worked out better than I ever imagined.

Once I had established a plan, there was clear work to be done, clear investment that needed made, clear channels for time and effort, and everyone knew what return was expected. It turned out that a couple of the companies I was building plans for ended up doing great business with specialty marketing companies, and another one made a fantastic full-time hire...and the new person knew what they were supposed to be doing! Within my own company, I put someone to work on the marketing who wasn't me, since I had a clear plan and actions steps instead of just ideas.

If you're interested in getting that plan, just contact me. I like sharing it.

TEMPLATE EVERYTHING YOU CAN

Marketing plans used to feel way over my head but now they're easy, because there's a template for that in my arsenal of tools. In fact, there are many things that are easy for me now that were really difficult before. These things aren't easy just because I'm experienced... I've had plenty of experience getting a drink out of my kitchen, but I still walk out of there once a week with a sandwich on accident. Experience helps, but it's definitely not the only thing I rely on. The work that I'm talking about has become easy because I made templates for how to do it. I have a go-to budget template, a go-to contract template, a go-to assessment template. I've even created a system for how I wash my hands in restrooms with motion detected towel dispensers.

Pro tip: Wave your hand before you wash, then hold your hands in front of the sensor while using the first towel. It'll make you feel so efficient.

That does NOT mean my creativity has been stifled. On the contrary, it means that space now exists to be *more* creative. If you're not spending time re-building all the parts you've already built before, it means that you now have time to innovate new things. How often do you have deep thoughts in the shower? Probably fairly often. That's because your brain gets to go on auto-pilot. Your brain knows how you take showers, you've done it a thousand times, and now you can think about other things while you go through the motions. You might even come up with improvements for how you shower! You can always be innovating. Use the free space that you've created through process to come up with even more improvements.

I've revised my budget template several times now. I had the time and headspace to do that because I had a template to build on. When I need to make a budget for someone, it can just be customized from my selection of what is already available, instead of re-creating it from scratch each time. It also means that I often get to step away from the entire thing and say, "If this should do X, can it be done on this foundation at all? Perhaps it <u>IS</u> time to build something completely new."

I should take a moment to point out what I am NOT saying. I am NOT saying that you should make things one-size-fits-all. One size does not fit all.

Making templates means that instead of going to each individual person and having a conversation about how to keep his or her feet warm, you can learn that socks help keep feet warm. Then you learn how to make socks, and make a template for sock-making. This will enable you to have a conversation about what size foot any person has and what colors they like, and tailor socks to each person. You'll also be able to quickly notice if they don't need socks at all and then be able to move on to other solutions.

Templates should give you more room to be creative. So template everything you can.

YOU CAN'T IMPROVE
ON NOTHING

In order to improve there must be something to improve upon. How many first impressions do you get with someone? Just one of course. So it has to be perfect, right?

I just talked about making templates for things and how building from an existing foundation allows you to grow in an effective way... but building from a foundation means that there must be a foundation there to build on. Since you can't *build up* to your first impression, it must be the first impression that *is* the foundation.

I once heard Tony Robbins say that, "Style is the most important thing...initially." I'm not sure if he took that quote from someone else because we've all heard something like that before. Perhaps you've heard it this way: *Beauty is only skin deep.* The point is that you should work hard to make a good first impression, but that's only going to get you to the next thirty seconds or, if you have a great first impression, the first meeting or two. After that it's about the value you bring and the substance underneath the skin.

In sales, over and over, you're establishing relationships in order to exchange value with each other. Relationships are built. The first impression helps but there are an endless supply of stories about terrible first meetings that, through some persistence and intention, turned into wonderful relationships. They were improved upon!

That's why you cannot simply do nothing and expect to make a good first impression with someone and have everything happen all at once. While you'll find the occasional customer that knows exactly what they want right off the bat, it's likely that you'll have a lot of them (read: most) who you'll need to connect with multiple times. You have to start the relationship and then improve upon it, and you can't improve on nothing.

EVERY CONVERSATION

I talk a lot about how people are people. I talk about business being simply trading value between relationships, and about how a genuine connection will take you the furthest. But what if you don't have any relationships at all? A book I once read talked about how the biggest, most important step I had to take in finding great new relationships was to let go of all the ones I didn't like having. I remember thinking "I can't let them go...*I don't HAVE any*."

I'm not going to talk about the *specific methods* of how to get customers and relationships because that changes all the time. It can change by the decade, or the business type, or the product, and sometimes by the phase of the moon. What I am going to say is this: you're not going to make any new relationships or get any value traded with those relationships if you're not having any conversations.

The other day my friend (an engineer doing outside sales) and I were talking about how he took what would have been a sale for one of

Widget A, and instead got a sale of *ninety* of Widget B. I'm saying widget because the stuff he sells is way over my head and I don't really know what any of it is. Something about scanning machines and code readers. The point is that the person purchasing didn't know that Widget B existed...but it's what his company *actually* needed. My friend changed everything because he had a conversation.

You have to have conversations in order to get sales. In sales, do you know what the difference is between the first "first conversation" you have with someone and the 10,000th "first conversation" you have with someone is? 9,999 other people know you exist. As of this writing there are about seven billion "first conversations" that you could have this year just to make everyone aware that your product exists, let alone talking about whether it might be valuable to anyone.

There are plenty of ways to "target your customers" or "talk to decision makers", etc. But the reality is that unless you're having some conversations, you're not going anywhere.

YOUR DREAM 100

In the book *The Ultimate Sales Machine,* author Chet Holmes introduces the concept of the Dream 100. I want to really bring this concept to bear because I've seen how effective it is. The idea is this: Pick your top 100 working relationships that it would be a dream to have and then pointedly have conversations with them non-stop until you find a way to do business. You might be at that for a week and you might be at it for five years.

The idea sounds a little crazy, especially since the cultural standard right now is to do your marketing and wait to see who becomes a customer. Since I've spent the entirety of this book bucking that idea it follows that I'd keep doing it here.

Some people might go a step beyond marketing their product and even offer to do some sort of "solution/need fit" analysis. Perhaps they do this even before they reach out to have a conversation. I've coached a few clients that researched and scored a company's online presence   and only reach out if that company scores below a certain threshold. Meaning their target is clearly someone who could use their solution. Even within my own company we offer a free mini-assessment for businesses and a free thirty minute consultation to see if we could be a good fit. But even all of that isn't what I'm talking about.

For the Dream 100, we're talking about something different. You should take your product, figure out how it will work for your dream 100, and then continue asking those companies for work/partnership/sales. You should be asking, and asking again, and again, and again. This is like the email that pops up in your inbox every week for a year before you click on it. The Facebook ad that you can't ignore anymore, and the guy who invites you to bowling league every second Tuesday for five years. This is persistence with intention.

Remember too that this continues even if you're rejected, which is a wholly terrifying thought. In the world of dating, this idea is what produces either the absolute best or worst stories. The worst stories are the ones about stalkers. If you become a marketing machine that doesn't understand "just being friends" it's going to get ugly; however, if you let them live, and simply continue to be a constant useful presence in their lives, then you have the opportunity to create a story that sounds more like this:

"Yeah, we knew each other for five years and they asked me out once a month. Never pushy, never upset, but never gave up. I finally gave in and of course here we are, still together and happy ten years later. They knew what they wanted and never gave up! Honestly, it was a little flattering."

You can have *that* story. Pick your Dream 100 and make them special. Pursue them kindly, consistently, and helpfully... but pursue. Like the rest of your dreams, don't give up just because someone doesn't see the value right away.

THE PRODUCT PYRAMID

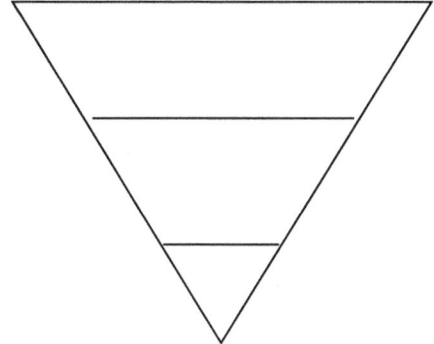

We all want our products to sell really well, right? Understanding the *product pyramid* will help that happen for you. I'm going to unpack this concept for a second, so hang with me.

First things first, the product pyramid is upside down. It's like a funnel, except I really dislike comparing things to funnels. Anyway, it should make sense when I talk about it as long as you remember to picture an upside down pyramid.

It's safe to assume that everyone needs air. Well, that's the top level of the pyramid. It's something that can be relevant across a broad spectrum.

Certainly everyone wants clean air, but simply taking a glance at China and L.A lets us know that there are quite a few people who aren't willing to pay the cost of having it. It doesn't matter how much it could improve their lives or how much better it might be for them, it's just not important enough. So, "clean" air is actually for a more *narrow* audience.

What about scented air? Air that smells like mint, lavender, or apple pie. A smaller group of people are going to want a scent in their air. Even smaller groups of people will want *specific* scents.

With each extra thing, you're traveling down the pyramid to the more narrow sections at the bottom. "BUT IT'S AIR!" you might say, "everyone needs it!" Yes, but it's *"clean"* air that's tinted green and smells like cherries. You're going to have a very, very specific set of people who want that.

That's the product pyramid, and you have to decide what part of it you're going to focus on. Here's the deal: the higher up the (upside-down) pyramid your product is, the easier it is for someone else to provide and the cheaper it gets. BUT, it has mass appeal. The opposite is also true: the narrower you get the harder things become to provide and they become more valuable... but only for a very narrow set of people.

Also, things become more valuable by factors. What I mean is that the "everyone" that wants and needs air isn't really all that interested in how they get it or what form it comes in. But when you get to the very narrow spot the people in it are nearly fanatical about their thing. Think about the levels coffee has been taken to in the last few decades. It's practically cultish when you reach the tiny point of the pyramid that includes the pour-over-no-cream-no-sugar-served-with-a-bean-on-the-side individual.

Did you know there is such a thing as bespoke jeans? "Bespoke" means made from scratch. These jeans are intimately customized. You can buy a pair of Wrangler jeans at Wal-Mart for what, thirty dollars? Bespoke jeans cost upwards of $1,200. Bespoke Jeans have a tiny, fanatical fan base.

Each time you add another qualifier to your product the audience gets narrower, but also that much more dedicated and invested.

I've seen a lot of businesses provide ten products, all in the widest part, and then wonder why they can't reach their "target" audience. Or it's completely the opposite, with someone wondering why a hand-blown gold-rimmed snifter isn't appealing to the masses.

In the best interests of everyone, let's consider the upside down pyramid and use it to sell really well to the people who care.

TARGETS AND SPHERES

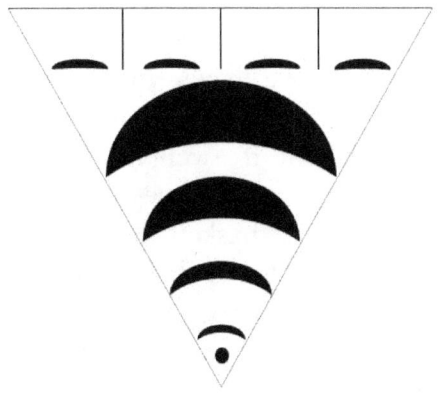

Yes, this graphic is strange and, no, I don't expect it to make any sense before I explain it. When images like this appear on the whiteboard next to my desk at home my wife calls them my "master's thesis as art."

What I intend to convey is that targeting specific markets is the best way to go about making sales (relationships), and that doing so will give you the influence you need to expand effectively into new markets.

The triangle portion of this image has the same concept as the product pyramid. As you travel down the pyramid, the audience becomes smaller and smaller. In this same way we talk about the shrinking size of target markets.

I want to point out that in the image above, there are multiple different arcs. Each of these arcs represents a "target market" or a market segment. Obviously, it starts tiny at the bottom and the markets keep growing as you move upwards. This might mean that in the very smallest section we have: men, living in the United States, specifically Illinois and Indiana, who are twenty-one to twenty-five, over six feet tall, and are Juniors in college. This might be similar to a college basketball recruiter's search criteria. It's possible to be extremely specific about who it is you're trying to sell to, and being specific is usually the smartest place to start.

Each broader arc, or segment, means that you expand out to a broader market. You normally want to do that when you've looked through most of the people who fit the description of the current market, and you want to try a new market. The second layer does not include Juniors, since you've already looked at most of those, but it looks at the broader market of Freshman and Sophomores. Then, perhaps having exhausted all of the kids in their first three years of college who are over six feet tall, we expand the search to those between five and six feet. You don't include the "over six footers" in your new market because you've already scouted those, but it's still a bigger market, even without them, because there are a lot of men in Illinois and Indiana between twenty-one and twenty-five who aren't quite six feet tall.

Now that I've explained market segments let's talk about spheres of influence and why it's best practice to start with a small, specific segment and work your way outward.

In the graphic, at the very tip of the triangle, is a small black dot. This represents your sphere of influence in that segment. You'll notice that the dot does not take up very much room, and that is because your sphere of influence is small when you start, even in a tiny market. You'll also notice that the segment itself isn't very big, which means that you don't have to make too many more relationships before your sphere of influence could expand to cover it.

Each segment, as you go towards larger and larger markets, has a black portion in it already. This black portion represents the amount of influence that you're likely to have in your new market, assuming you capture the majority of the segment before it. As you go upwards into larger markets, your sphere of influence is a larger and larger portion.

Since I believe understanding *why* things happen is important, we'll jump into the those factors:

lessening degrees of connection, and word of mouth referral.

Lessening degrees of connection means that each time you move into a new market, you bring all the relationships you've already built along with you.

As an example, let us say the smallest segment is Brian, and you get to know him. When you move to the new, larger segment of Tom, there's a possibility that Brian already knows Tom. If he does, since you already know Tom's friend it's a lot easier for you to make a relationship with Tom. You get to start the Tom market with lot of influence already in place. You might have experienced this if you've ever met someone and they said to you "Oh yes, I know you, Jane talks about you all the time."

That is lessening degrees of connection in action. Simply, the more people you know, the more people you're only a single step away from. In our culture today, there is nowhere we're able to experience this on a more tangible level than LinkedIn. The website actually shows *exactly* how many relationship steps, or degrees of connection, you are from another person.

Now to talk about **Word of mouth influence**. Once you know Brian and Tom, you might expand to the very broad market of David. In this new market, you actually have even *more* influence than you did before. You have less degrees of connection, and Brain and Tom both know about you, which means they might share stories about you. Since Brian and Tom share stories with each other while they're around David, it means that there's a pretty good chance that David has heard about you from his friends. This is word of mouth influence. Word of mouth is important when it comes from a single person, but the effect is more powerful by factors when it's a shared experience that people get to communicate about together.

As you saturate a smaller market and move on to larger ones, you carry the influence with you from both of these effects and you start in new markets with a greater sphere.

THIS MEANS YOU HAVE TO BE REALLY CAREFUL!

Imagine this for just a moment as a warning: what if you're not a very nice person to have a relationship with? What if you force sell to people, and you sell a product that isn't very good or doesn't live up to the expectations that you set? Every time you do that and burn another bridge, you're effectively growing your sphere of *negative* influence. We'll talk about the gimmick in just a minute but, this is why new methods of selling get introduced and work amazingly well for only a very short amount of time. It doesn't take very long for people to communicate with each other about their bad experience. There's a reason the saying goes, "it spread like wildfire."

The portion of the image at the very top represents new but disconnected markets. Here's what I mean by that: at some point, you'll make your market so large that you have to start over, because your markets simply don't reach any further. This might be represented best in our previous example of the basketball recruiter by zooming all the way out to the level of the United States market. Now that you know every kid who's eligible to play basketball in the whole United States, it's time to start looking at other countries. The problem is, your entire massive market isn't very likely to have ever established relationships with people in those other countries. There simply aren't very many relationships for you to use as a bridge. So, you have to start narrowing down what you're looking for again, and then out of your massive market influence, you'll find that you have little bits of influence within each of your brand new segments.

Phew, I don't know if I've done justice to this topic, but I think that I've done my absolute best short of writing that thesis paper, so I hope that this all makes enough sense for you to understand the importance in sales of choosing a specific market, and also of building great relationships with those people.

DON'T GIVE IN
TO THE GIMMICK

Alright, I admit it: I'm a planner, an organizer, and a structure builder. I demand process, order, and constant improvement. There's a powerful skill in all of those things but there's an even more powerful danger. *I find it so much easier to invest my time in changing systems than producing results.* Almost always I experience a split between being uncomfortable with the work, or having my planning side take over and get excited about finding more ways to improve. It has nothing to do with working, it has everything to do with the type of work.

I really enjoy talking to people, but I have a hard time thinking of anything that makes me exhausted faster. So whenever I hear someone say "We can increase your sales by 300% with our amazing system!" I click. I pay attention because making a process better is exciting to me, and it definitely takes less energy than *actually talking to people*. (Go figure right?) It's always the same though: *"Pay hundreds of dollars for us to tell you how to make a list that says to have 5 conversations every day!"*

I always click because I don't want to face reality: There is no gimmick. There is no secret formula, there is no golden ticket, and there is no magical phrase that will suddenly make the whole process run without people involved. There is only hard work. There is only having conversations with real people every, single, day.

Every sales book that I've read talks about the different methods for having conversations. All the different types of sales pitch, phrasing and arts of conversation. You know what that means, right? Every book assumes that you're having conversations.

As the world has become digital, the value of a genuine conversation has not gone anywhere. Communicating with each other is a basic human function and it won't be going anywhere as long as we're human. If that part ever changes I'll probably have to make a few other edits to the book anyway.

This reality goes both ways in conversation. Just like you shouldn't fall for the gimmick, you shouldn't put one out there for other people to fall for. For all the information and data that we have the goal of all of our websites and books is to be as human as possible. They should answer, as simply as possible, every question that someone needs to ask before purchasing a product. The best websites say exactly what they represent within a few seconds. You have to be as genuine as possible, as fast as possible. If you can cut out ALL the fluff then you're doing well. Which is why this book is so short, obviously!

We have a "snake oil" perception of sales people, which means we perceive that they're selling something useless as if it's really valuable. We have a general dispassion for when people talk up their product like we're not, or cannot be, informed about what exactly it is and how it will benefit us.

When you're having genuine conversations with people you learn how to be just like a website: clear, precise, and capable of answering questions.

Know what makes me the most frustrated though? For a while the gimmick actually works, and that's part of the deception. "Use this method for guaranteed results!" That's what you hear, and they even show you success! It seems so simple! And then it all falls apart because the method was a gimmick and now people know about the gimmick and they hate you for using it and your sales are awful even if your product is good because they can't trust you.

Don't fall for the gimmick.
Always be having conversations.
Always be genuine.
Always be human.

ABOUT THE AUTHOR

Nathan Young is a Husband, Father, Friend, Student, and Business Owner, in that order, whether he remembers it every day or not.

He is a human, and he wants to meet you if you are too. He would like to help and to learn from you as much as possible.

Don't hesitate to reach out to him

www.ingramcontent.com/pod-product-compliance
Lightning Source LLC
Chambersburg PA
CBHW070135210526
45170CB00013B/1087